T0009896

UNPLUG

UNPLUG

Meditations
& Inspirations

MANDALA

San Rafael · Los Angeles · London

Most people's minds are almost always TOO BUSY for them to feel their skin being caressed by the wind or the sun.

—MOKOKOMA MOKHONOANA

We live in a world where there is more and more INFORMATION, and less and less MEANING.

—JEAN BAUDRILLARD

At home,
surrounded by
information,
by screens,
I am no longer
ANYWHERE,
but rather
EVERYWHERE,
in the midst of a
universal banality.

To arrive in a new city, or in a new language, is suddenly to find oneself here and nowhere else.

—JEAN BAUDRILLARD

This wasted time
I have found to
be by constant
experience to be
as indispensable
AS SLEEP.

—JOHN ADAMS

Where are
we to put the
limit between
the body and
THE WORLD,
since the world
is flesh?

—MAURICE
MERLEAU-PONTY

The saddest aspect of life right now is that science gathers KNOWLEDGE faster than society gathers WISDOM.

—ISAAC ASIMOV

I tried to discover, in the rumor of forests and waves, words that other men could not hear,

and I pricked up my ears to listen to the revelation of their harmony.

—GUSTAVE FLAUBERT

A point of
view can be a
DANGEROUS
luxury when
substituted
for insight and
understanding.

—MARSHALL MCLUHAN

The camera
makes everyone
A TOURIST
in other people's
reality, and
eventually in
one's own.

—SUSAN SONTAG

Man was not
meant to live
at the speed
OF LIGHT.

—MARSHALL MCLUHAN

Cherish that which is within you, and shut off that which IS WITHOUT.

—CHUANG TZU

Begin doing
what you want
to do now.
We are not living
in ETERNITY.

We have only
this MOMENT,
sparkling like a
star in our hand
—and melting like
a snowflake . . .

—FRANCIS BACON

LIFE MUST BE LIVED AS PLAY.

—PLATO

Lack of
DIRECTION,
not lack
OF TIME,
is the problem.

—ZIG ZIGLAR

A man who
dares to waste
one hour of
time has not
discovered the
value of life.

—CHARLES DARWIN

To make the right choices in life, you have to get in touch with your soul.

To do this,
you need to
experience
SOLITUDE.

—DEEPAK CHOPRA

Sometimes
sitting and doing
NOTHING
is the best
SOMETHING
you can do.

—KAREN SALMANSOHN

You can
never get a
cup of tea
large enough
or a book
long enough
to suit me.

—C. S. LEWIS

HAPPINESS
is not something
ready-made.
It comes from
your own actions.

—DALAI LAMA XIV

How different
would people act
if they couldn't
show off on
social media?

Would they
still do it?

—DONNA LYNN HOPE

Thousands
of tired,
nerve-shaken,
over-civilized
people are
beginning to

find out that
going to the
mountains is
going HOME;
that wildness is
a NECESSITY.

—JOHN MUIR

The greatest
power one
human being
can exert over
others is to
control their
perceptions
of reality,

and infringe on
the integrity
and individuality
of their world.

—PHILIP K. DICK

Not just
BEAUTIFUL,
though—the
stars are like
the trees in the
forest, alive
and breathing.

And they're
watching me.

—HARUKI MURAKAMI

Everything in nature invites us constantly to be what WE ARE.

—GRETEL EHRLICH

You leave old habits behind by starting out with the thought, "I release the need for this in my life."

—WAYNE DYER

The mind is its
OWN PLACE,
and in it self

Can make a
Heav'n of Hell,
a Hell of Heav'n.

—JOHN MILTON

These days
UNPLUGGED
places are
getting hard
to find.

—RICHARD LOUV

Being
connected to
everything has
disconnected
us from
OURSELVES.

—L. M. BROWNING

My wish simply
is to live my life
as fully as I can.
In both our work
and our leisure, I
think, we should
be so employed.

And in our time
this means that
we must save
ourselves from
the products
that we are asked
to buy in order,
ultimately, to
replace ourselves.

—WENDELL BERRY

I spent a
LIFETIME
in a garden one
AFTERNOON.

—CRAIG D.
LOUNSBROUGH

The soul
should always
stand ajar,
ready to welcome
the ecstatic
EXPERIENCE.

—EMILY DICKINSON

What do you
mean you've
been spying on
me, with this
thing in my hand
that is an eye?

—PATRICIA LOCKWOOD

The PAST has no power over the PRESENT moment.

—ECKHART TOLLE

For there is never anything but the PRESENT, and if one cannot live there, one cannot live ANYWHERE.

—ALAN WATTS

UNCHARTED TERRITORY IS A GOOD PLACE TO BE IN.

—BO BURNHAM

We live in
an age when
unnecessary
things are our
only necessities.

—OSCAR WILDE

[Electronic media]
is all cultural
DIVERSION,
and what is REAL
is you and your
friends and your
associations,

your highs, your
orgasms, your
hopes, your plans,
your fears.

—TERENCE MCKENNA

There is a
pleasure in the
pathless woods,

There is a
rapture on the
lonely shore,

There is society
where none
intrudes,

By the deep
Sea, and music
in its roar:

I love not Man
the less, but
Nature more . . .

—LORD BYRON

Until you realize
how easy it is
for your mind to
be manipulated,

you remain
the PUPPET
of someone
else's game.

—EVITA OCHEL

A scholar tries to LEARN something every day; a student of Buddhism tries to UNLEARN something daily.

—ALAN WATTS

Before you
become too
entranced
with gorgeous
gadgets and
mesmerizing
video displays,

let me remind
you that
information is
not knowledge,
knowledge is
not wisdom,
and wisdom is
not foresight.

—ARTHUR C. CLARKE

When you bow,
you should just
bow; when you
sit, you should
just sit; when
you eat, you
should just eat.

—SHUNRYU SUZUKI

We do well
to UNPLUG
regularly. Quiet
time restores
FOCUS and
composure.

—DANIEL GOLEMAN

Computers are
USELESS.
They can
only give you
ANSWERS.

—PABLO PICASSO

Walk as if you are KISSING the earth with your feet.

—THICH NHAT HANH

One day spent
with someone
you love
can change
EVERYTHING.

—MITCH ALBOM

Slow down and enjoy life. It's not only the scenery you miss by going too fast—you also miss the sense of where you are going and why.

—EDDIE CANTOR

My head'll
explode if I
continue with
this escapism.

—JESS C. SCOTT

In the spring, at the end of the day, you should smell like dirt.

—MARGARET ATWOOD

I have begun
to wonder if
the SECRET
of living well is
NOT in having
all the answers

but in
PURSUING
unanswerable
questions in
good company.

—RACHEL NAOMI REMEN

I only went out
for a walk and
finally concluded
to STAY OUT
till sundown,

for going out,
I found, was
really going in.

—JOHN MUIR

Nothing ever
becomes
real till it is
EXPERIENCED.

—JOHN KEATS

BOOKS
DON'T NEED
BATTERIES.

—Nadine Gordimer

We're plugged
in twenty-four
hours a day.
We're all part of
one big machine,
whether we
are conscious
of that or not.

And if we can't unplug from that machine, eventually we're going to become MINDLESS.

—ALAN LIGHTMAN

We live by a
PERCEPTUAL
"map" which
is never
REALITY itself.

—CARL R. ROGERS

Are you managing your ENERGY well and using it for things that MATTER?

Do you stop to recharge before you push yourself to critically low levels? UNPLUG to RECHARGE.

—SUSAN C. YOUNG

The present is all
we have, yet it
is the one thing
we will never
learn to HOLD
in our hands.

—MADELEINE THIEN

The longing for PARADISE is man's longing not to be man.

—MILAN KUNDERA

This society ELIMINATES geographical distance only to produce a new internal SEPARATION.

—GUY DEBORD

Death is no
more than
PASSING
from one room
into another.
But there's a
difference for
me, you know.

Because in
that other
room I shall be
able to SEE.

—HELEN KELLER

What the public wants is the image of PASSION, not passion itself.

—ROLAND BARTHES

SILENCE,
I learned, is
sometimes the
most beautiful
SOUND.

—CHARLOTTE ERIKSSON

Physical books
are tough, hard
to destroy,
bath-resistant,
solar-operated,
feel good
in your hand:

they are good
at being books,
and there will
always be a
place for them.

—NEIL GAIMAN

Sit down
before fact as
a little child,
be prepared to
give up every
preconceived
notion, follow
HUMBLY

wherever and
to whatever
abysses nature
leads, or you
shall learn
NOTHING.

—THOMAS HUXLEY

I don't need anyone else to distract me from myself anymore, like I always thought I would.

—CHARLOTTE ERIKSSON

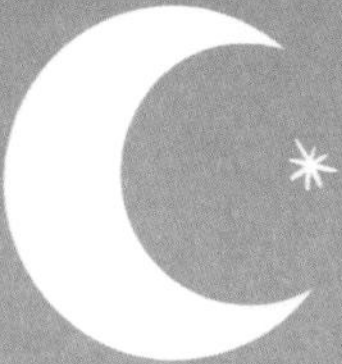

Whether you
EXPERIENCE
heaven or hell,
remember
that it is your
MIND which
creates them.

—TIMOTHY LEARY

But every time she remembered her phone wasn't there, she felt RELIEVED and FREE all over again.

Like she'd been
given more
LIFE TO LIVE.

—MEGAN ANGELO

Almost everything will work again if you UNPLUG it for a few minutes, including YOU.

—ANNE LAMOTT

One thing
about which fish
know exactly
nothing is water,
since they
have no anti-
environment

which would
enable them
to perceive
the element
they live in.

—MARSHALL MCLUHAN

THE FLESH
IS AT THE
HEART OF
THE WORLD.

—Maurice Merleau-Ponty

VISIBILITY IS A TRAP.

—Michel Foucault

Do stuff.
Be clenched,
CURIOUS.
Not waiting for
inspiration's shove
or society's kiss
on your forehead.

—SUSAN SONTAG

But I know, somehow, that only when it is DARK enough can you see the STARS.

—MARTIN LUTHER KING JR.

Beware the
BARRENNESS
of a busy life.

—SOCRATES

Take no one's
word for
ANYTHING,
including mine—
but trust your
EXPERIENCE.

—JAMES BALDWIN

I'll tell you what
hermits realize:
if you go off into
a far forest and
get very quiet,

you'll come
to understand
that you're
connected with
EVERYTHING.

—ALAN WATTS

There's a special phenomenology to walking in woods in winter.

—HELEN MACDONALD

If we don't know how to be ALONE, we'll only know how to be LONELY.

—SHERRY TURKLE

ALWAYS SAY
"YES" TO
THE PRESENT
MOMENT.

Say "YES" to life and see how life suddenly starts working for you rather than against you.

—ECKHART TOLLE

Everything
has BEAUTY,
but not
everyone sees it.

—CONFUCIUS

I cannot
endure to
waste anything
so precious
as autumnal
SUNSHINE
by staying in
the house.

—NATHANIEL
HAWTHORNE

WHAT CONSUMES YOUR MIND CONTROLS YOUR LIFE.

—Unknown

The attempt
to ESCAPE
from pain is
what creates
more pain.

—GABOR MATÉ

Sometimes we spend so much time and energy thinking about where we want to go that we don't notice where we happen to be.

—DAN GUTMAN

We refuse to
turn off our
COMPUTERS
because in those
moments we

might actually
have to face
up to who we
REALLY ARE.

—JEFFERSON BETHKE

Even the
technology
that promises
to unite us,
DIVIDES US.

—DAN BROWN

BOREDOM
is not far from
bliss: it is bliss
seen from
the shores of
PLEASURE.

—ROLAND BARTHES

Perfection of
character is this:

to live each day
as if it were your
last, without
frenzy, without
apathy, without
PRETENSE.

—MARCUS AURELIUS

Technology is destructive only in the hands of people who do not realize that they are ONE and the same process as the UNIVERSE.

—ALAN WATTS

The real danger is not that computers will begin to think like men, but that men will begin to think like computers.

—SYDNEY HARRIS

It's bad for
your brain not
to UNPLUG.

—JOHN GREEN

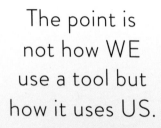

The point is
not how WE
use a tool but
how it uses US.

—NICK JOAQUIN

There are only
two ways to
live your life.
ONE is as
though nothing
is a miracle.

The OTHER
is as though
everything is
a miracle.

—ALBERT EINSTEIN

Should you shield
the canyons from
the windstorms,
you would never
SEE THE TRUE
BEAUTY of
their carvings.

—ELIZABETH
KÜBLER-ROSS

It's very, very
dangerous to
lose contact
with living
NATURE.

—ALBERT HOFMANN

Sometimes you have to disconnect in order to better connect with YOURSELF.

—RYAN HOLIDAY

I like living.
I have sometimes
been wildly,
despairingly,
acutely miserable,
racked with
sorrow;

but through it all
I still know quite
certainly that
just to be alive
is a grand thing.

—AGATHA CHRISTIE

What you're supposed to do when you don't like a thing is CHANGE IT.

If you can't change it, change the way you THINK about it. Don't complain.

MAYA ANGELOU

Sometimes our STOP-DOING list needs to be bigger than our TO-DO list.

—PATTI DIGH

Enjoy the peace
of Nature, and
declutter your
INNER WORLD.

—AMIT RAY

We can easily forgive a child who is afraid of the dark; the real tragedy of life is when men are afraid of the light.

—PLATO

Life isn't about
FINDING
yourself.
Life is about
CREATING
yourself.

—GEORGE
BERNARD SHAW

Get yourself
out of whatever
CAGE you
find yourself in.

—JOHN CAGE

This is the
whole point of
technology.
It creates an
APPETITE for
immortality on
the one hand.

It threatens
universal
EXTINCTION
on the other.
Technology is
lust removed
from nature.

—DON DELILLO

Sometimes
you need to sit
LONELY on the
floor in a quiet
room in order to
hear your own
voice and not let
it drown in the
noise of others.

—CHARLOTTE ERIKSSON

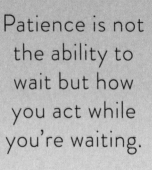

Patience is not the ability to wait but how you act while you're waiting.

—JOYCE MEYER

Boredom is the
dream bird that
hatches the egg
of experience.

—WALTER BENJAMIN

Unfortunately,
the clock is
ticking, the hours
are going by.

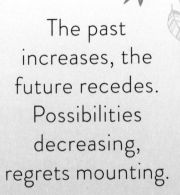

The past
increases, the
future recedes.
Possibilities
decreasing,
regrets mounting.

—HARUKI MURAKAMI

Soon silence
will have passed
into legend. Man
has turned his
back on silence.
Day after day
he invents
machines and
devices that

increase noise
and distract
humanity from the
essence of life,
contemplation,
MEDITATION.

—JEAN ARP

OUR TASK MUST
BE TO FREE
OURSELVES . . .

by widening
our circle of
COMPASSION
to embrace all
living creatures
and the whole
of nature and
its beauty.

—ALBERT EINSTEIN

The more I read, the more I acquire, the more certain I am that I know NOTHING.

—VOLTAIRE

It always
pays to dwell
slowly on the
BEAUTIFUL
things—the
more beautiful
the more slowly.

—ATTICUS

I believe in the value of the book, which keeps something irreplaceable,

and in the
NECESSITY
of fighting
to secure its
RESPECT.

—JACQUES DERRIDA

The primary
element in any
CIVILIZATION
is a stable
relation between
man and his
environment.

—JACQUES ELLUL

It was sunsets that taught me that beauty sometimes only lasts for a couple of MOMENTS,

and it was
sunrises that
showed me that
all it takes is
PATIENCE to
experience it
all over again.

—A. J. LAWLESS

The more ways
we have to
CONNECT,
the more many
of us seem
desperate to
UNPLUG.

—PICO IYER

MAY YOU
LIVE EVERY
DAY OF
YOUR LIFE.

—Jonathan Swift

It's only after
you've stepped
outside your
comfort zone
that you begin
to change,
grow, and
TRANSFORM.

—ROY T. BENNETT

Adopt the
pace of nature:
her secret is
PATIENCE.

—RALPH WALDO
EMERSON

But man is a
part of nature,
and his war
against nature
is inevitably
a war against
HIMSELF.

—RACHEL CARSON

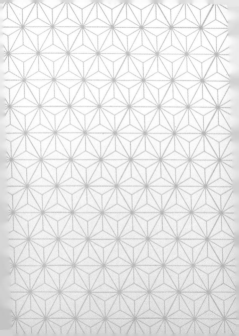

I have
nature and art
and poetry,
and if that is
not enough,
what is enough?

—VINCENT VAN GOGH

Please, no matter how we advance technologically, please don't abandon the BOOK.

There is nothing
in our material
world more
beautiful than
the book.

—PATTI SMITH

Technology is the knack of so arranging the world that we do not experience it.

—ROLLO MAY

"DIGIPHRENIA" —the way our media and technologies encourage us to be in more than one place at the same time.

–DOUGLAS RUSHKOFF

Realize deeply that the present moment is all you have. Make the NOW the primary focus of your life.

—ECKHART TOLLE

Those who are able to see BEYOND the shadows and lies of their culture will never be UNDERSTOOD, let alone believed, by the masses.

—PLATO

A quiet and
modest life
brings more
JOY than
a pursuit of
success bound
with constant
UNREST.

—ALBERT EINSTEIN

TO FIND
YOURSELF,
THINK FOR
YOURSELF.

—Socrates

As the world grows ever more CLAMOROUS, my hunger for silence steepens.

—JANE HIRSHFIELD

The lake and
the mountains
have become
my landscape,
my real world.

—GEORGE SIMENON

People are so
busy chasing
happiness—if
they would slow
down and turn
around they
would give it a
chance to catch
up with them.

—HAROLD S. KUSHNER

YOU MAY
DELAY,
BUT TIME
WILL NOT.

—Benjamin Franklin

My NEW
deliberate and
slower pace has
created a higher
QUALITY in
my experiences.

—LISA J. SHULTZ

How could they see anything but the SHADOWS if they were never allowed to move their HEADS?

—PLATO

I felt my lungs
inflate with
the onrush of
SCENERY:

air, mountains,
trees, people.
I thought,
"This is what it
is to be happy."

—SYLVIA PLATH

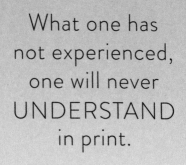

What one has
not experienced,
one will never
UNDERSTAND
in print.

—ISADORA DUNCAN

Nowhere can
a man find a
quieter or more
UNTROUBLED
retreat than in
his own soul.

—MARCUS AURELIUS

MEDITATION
is the ultimate
mobile device;
you can use
it anywhere,
ANYTIME,
unobtrusively.

—SHARON SALZBERG

DISTRACTED
from
DISTRACTION
by
DISTRACTION.

—T.S. ELIOT

I find it
REFRESHING
to unplug from it
for a while. You
kind of forget how
deeply you get
embedded in it.

—WILL WRIGHT

Every second
spent staring at
the screen was
a second spent
rejecting LIFE.

—A. D. ALIWAT

Risks must
be TAKEN
because the
greatest hazard
in life is to risk
NOTHING.

—LEO BUSCAGLIA

From this point
forth, find me
nowhere,

Socially unseen,

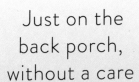

Just on the
back porch,
without a care

And without
a screen

—ERIC OVERBY

I think it pisses
GOD off if you
walk by the color
purple in a field
somewhere and
don't notice it.

—ALICE WALKER

Your vision will become CLEAR only when you can look INTO your own heart.

Who looks outside, dreams; who looks inside, AWAKES.

—CARL JUNG

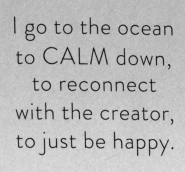

I go to the ocean
to CALM down,
to reconnect
with the creator,
to just be happy.

—NNEDI OKORAFOR

The world's big,
and I want to
have a good look
at it before it
gets DARK.

—JOHN MUIR

We should look WITHIN; the paths of the heart lead to nearby UNIVERSES full of life and affection for humanity.

—TERENCE MCKENNA

The nurse of
full-grown souls
is SOLITUDE.

—JAMES RUSSELL
LOWELL

There's a beauty to WISDOM and experience that cannot be faked. It's impossible to be mature without having LIVED.

—AMY GRANT

Mandala Publishing
P.O. Box 3088
San Rafael, CA 94912
www.mandalaearth.com

Find us on Facebook: www.facebook.com/MandalaEarth
Follow us on Twitter: @MandalaEarth
Follow us on Instagram: @MandalaEarth

CEO: Raoul Goff
Editorial Director: Katie Killebrew
VP Creative: Chrissy Kwasnik
VP Manufacturing: Alix Nicholaeff
Associate Art Director: Ashley Quackenbush
Designer: Lola Villanueva
Project Editor: Claire Yee
Editorial Assistant: Sophia R Wright
Production Associate: Andy Harper

ISBN: 978-1-64722-643-5
Manufactured in China by Insight Editions
10 9 8 7 6 5 4 3 2 1
2022 2023 2024

Also available:
Unplug: A Day and Night Reflection Journal
ISBN: 978-1-68383-998-9